SSSSSSSH!

The Word of the Lord

Shall Prevail

D1565166

Rev. Betty Jean Hargis Kemper

SSSSSSSH! The Word of the Lord Shall Prevail
Copyright © July 2015 by Rev. Betty Hargis Kemper

Printed in USA

Dedication

This book is dedicated to my children and my grandchildren. This book is also dedicated in loving memory to my parents, Reverend Winston and Lilly Hargis, and my father-in-law, Harold Kemper.

PREFACE

First of all, I would like to thank my sister, Della, who had the vision for me to write this book of encouragement. Della has published two books already with the help of her son, Robert.

The importance of the Word of God was taught to me as a child at my Father's and Mother's knees. Later, as I grew in wisdom and stature with the Lord, I discovered how much I needed to study and incorporate God's Word into my everyday life.

My goal is to convince you that God's Word will prevail in your life at all times. I will share testimonies from my own life, from the lives of others, and from the Bible when the Word of the Lord prevailed. Why can we boldly and confidently know that the title of this book is true? The reason is that we know God, we know God's word is true and we know the words of Jesus in John 15:7 (NKJV) which states, "If you abide in me, and My words abide in you, you will ask what you desire and it shall be done." This is one way we can glorify our heavenly Father. My desire is that you will know God in a greater dimension than you did before you read this book. I pray that the Holy Spirit will guide you as you read and you will mix the word with faith and receive all that God desires for you.

As a diamond reflects all the beauty of the gem, it is God's desire that we reflect all the beauty of our Heavenly Father and our Savior Jesus Christ by the power of the Holy Spirit. The only way we can do this is to know God and that means knowing God's Word.

Let us begin our journey now.

Chapter 1

SSSSSSSH! The Word of the Lord Shall Prevail

First, let me explain our title. The Bible is the Word of the Lord. The Lord gave me this message during a very troubling time in my life. When I say SSSSSSSH!, I am talking to myself. When I say the Word of the Lord, I am referring to the Bible and the fact that the Holy Spirit and the Word are always in agreement.

Hebrews 4:12 (NKJV): "For the Word of God *is* living and powerful, and sharper than any two-edged sword, piercing even to the division of soul and spirit, and of joints and marrow, and is a discerner of the thoughts and intents of the heart."

I will tell you what happened to me and then tell you more about the word "prevail."

We know that the battlefield is in the mind. When negative thoughts run rampant in our minds, or when a doctor gives us a bad report, we stop it by saying to ourselves SSSSSSSH!

After I had been in the hospital for three days, I returned home and was recovering on the sofa. I began to shake and fear was tormenting me. I said, "SSSSSSSH!, Shut Up, Betty." Immediately, my mind was clear. When your mind is thinking all of those negative thoughts, it is not easy to stop them. However, that day, God showed me the way. After I stilled my mind, then I could say, "God has not given me a spirit of fear, but of power, love and a sound mind." "By the stripes of Jesus, I am healed." Now, by faith I could stop those fiery darts in my mind and my own thoughts. I was able to think clearly and spoke to myself, "Betty Jean, you were monitored three days in the hospital. Your heart, blood pressure and your stomach was pronounced healed by the Doctor's. The Doctor said you are perfect. This attack is not from God."

My husband, who was in the recliner next to me on the sofa, did not have a clue about the battle raging within me. I knew this battle was between God and me. I knew that God had already won so I only had to rest in His Word. I had to wait for God's Word to prevail (to triumph) in my life.

It is important to me that you know the details of when the Holy Spirit gave me this revelation. Let us delve deeper into the word "prevail."

Prevail means to endure. 1 Peter 1:25a (NIV): "The Word of the Lord endures forever." Prevail means to be victorious. A few synonyms include win, come out on top, succeed, prove superior over, conquer and overcome.

Jesus is our greatest example of someone who prevailed. Therefore, in Christ, we are victorious. In Christ, we win. In Christ, we triumph. In Christ, we come out on top. In Christ, we succeed. In Christ, we prove superior over. In and through Christ, we conquer and overcome. That is a reason to rejoice!

If all of this is true, and it is, then what do we do when the devil comes as a roaring lion, seeking whom he may devour? We stand still and see the salvation of God. We quiet our minds with a SSSSSSSH! We declare that the Word of the Lord shall prevail.

Like God told Joshua, we must meditate on the Word day and night!

1 Peter 5:8-11(NKJV): "Be sober, be vigilant because your adversary the devil walks about LIKE a roaring lion, seeking whom he may devour. Resist him, steadfast in the faith, knowing that the same sufferings are experienced by your brotherhood in the world. May the God of all

grace, who called us to His eternal glory by Christ Jesus after you have suffered a while, perfect, establish, strengthen and settle you. To Him, be the glory and the dominion forever and ever. Amen."

When we know that God has completed his work, we can enter into His rest. We say, "Yes Lord," to Your will and to Your way. When we encounter opposition of any kind, we can go immediately to God. Sometimes, we might have to say SSSSSSSH! The Word of the Lord shall prevail. We then proceed to sing to the Lord and make melody in our hearts to the Lord because Praise silences the enemy.

The truth is the highest realm of reality. Maybe your body hurts, but the truth is by the stripes of Jesus, we are healed. We need to declare the truth, the Word of the Lord.

Daily devotions are so important. A Daily Bible Reading plan is available and I have it on my computer. I cannot over emphasize the importance of daily Bible reading.

Many years ago, Rusty and I were attending a business conference in Las Vegas. He had to leave early for a meeting and asked me to take a taxi and meet him at the conference room at noon.

My prior knowledge told me that Las Vegas is a wicked, sinful place and fear tried to grip my heart and mind. Again, I knew I would need to talk to my Abba Father. I put that thought away and began to read my daily devotions. I was reading Song of Solomon 6:10 (KJV): "Who is she that looketh forth as the morning, fair as the moon and clear as the sun, and terrible as an army with banners." The Holy Spirit said in his still small voice, "That is who God's church is. Are you part of God's church?" "Yes," I said. Then I heard God say, "Go forth in faith and be who I made you to be." Immediately I was overcome with faith and was filled with joy. The joy of the Lord is our strength. To my delight, my taxi driver was a man of God and we talked about God the whole journey. There are Christians in Las Vegas!

Why can we boldly and confidently say, SSSSSSSH! The Word of the Lord Shall Prevail? One of the main reasons is because we know God and we know all that Christ has given to us. We have the knowledge of God. To know God, we can say to ourselves: SSSSSSSH! Be quiet, stop talking. Stop thinking. We quiet our minds so that our mouth and heart and mind line up only with the Word of the Lord. The knowledge of God is a wonderful thing and it means knowing God's Word. Because we know God and have the true knowledge of who God is, we know His Word is true. To know God means we will have faith in God. We must see the answer. Then we speak the answer, not the problem.

Proverbs 3:5-6 (AMP): "Lean on, trust in and be confident in the Lord with all your heart and mind and do not rely on your own insight or understanding. In all your ways, KNOW, recognize and acknowledge Him and He will direct and make straight and plain your paths."

Jeremiah 17:5-7 (NJKV): "Thus says the LORD: "Cursed *is* the man who trusts in man And makes flesh his strength, Whose heart departs from the LORD. For he shall be like a shrub in the desert, And shall not see when good comes, But shall inhabit the parched places in the wilderness, *In* a salt land *which is* not inhabited. "Blessed *is* the man who trusts in the LORD, And whose hope is the LORD,"

When we are tempted to put our trust in man, we decline. As for me and my house, we will trust in the Lord.

Did you know that even if you are walking through an illness, or waiting for the manifestation of healing to come, God can still use you? It happened to me. During one of my wilderness experiences, God gave me a dream. I did not think God could use me then, but it isn't based on us. It is resting on God's shoulders. The Word says that we never cease from yielding fruit. We are like a tree planted by the waters, which spreads out its roots by the river.

In the dream, God told me to go see a nephew and share the plan of salvation with him and he would be saved. I obeyed the Lord and took my nephew out to the beach to share the way of salvation.

When we arrived, it was extremely windy. Nevertheless, we rolled down the windows and I turned off the engine. I explained to him that I would like to share the plan of salvation. He agreed and let me know that his wedding was just around the corner. He told me that his precious bride wanted him to receive Jesus into his heart because she did not want them unequally yoked.

Acts 2:21 (KJV): "And it shall come to pass, whosoever shall call on the name of the Lord shall be saved." Romans 10:9-10 (KJV): "If thou shalt confess with thy mouth the Lord Jesus and shalt believe in thine heart that God hath raised him from the dead thou shalt be saved. For with the heart man believeth unto righteousness, and with the mouth confession is made unto salvation."

I said, "If you were the only one on the earth, Christ would have died for you. For God so loved the world that He gave His only begotten son that whosoever believeth in Him should not perish but have everlasting life." He said, "Lord, I repent and I ask you to come into my heart." I let him know that the angels were rejoicing because he had come home to Jesus. As we basked in the presence of the Lord, immediately the wind stopped blowing and there was a Holy calm.

When we have the knowledge of God, we are armed and ready for battle!

Romans 11:33-36 (AMP): "Oh, the depth of the riches and wisdom and knowledge of God! How unfathomable (inscrutable, unsearchable) are His judgments (His decisions)! And how untraceable (mysterious, undiscoverable) are His ways (His methods, His paths)!
34 For who has known the mind of the Lord *and* who has understood His thoughts, or who has [ever] been His counselor?
35 Or who has first given God anything that he might be paid back *or* that he could claim a recompense?

[36] For from Him and through Him and to Him are all things. [For all things originate with Him and come from Him; all things live through Him, and all things center in and tend to consummate and to end in Him.] To Him be glory forever! Amen (so be it)."

2 Corinthians 10:4-5 (NKJV): "For the weapons of our warfare are not carnal but mighty in God for pulling down strongholds, casting down arguments and every high thing that exalts itself against the knowledge of God, bringing every thought into captivity to the obedience of Christ and being ready to punish all disobedience when your obedience is fulfilled."

It is bringing every thought captive to the obedience of Christ.

Therefore, we have to stop those thoughts that are contrary to God's Word by saying, SSSSSSSH! The Word of the Lord Shall Prevail. Being obedient to God is so fulfilling. To know God is the greatest fulfillment in all the earth.

2 Corinthians 2:14-15 (AMP): "But thanks be to God, who in Christ always leads us in triumph as trophies of Christ's victory and through us spreads and makes evident the fragrance of the

15

KNOWLEDGE OF GOD EVERYWHERE, FOR WE ARE THE SWEET FRAGRANCE OF Christ which exhales unto God, discernible alike among those who are being saved and among those who are perishing."

Isaiah 50:7 (KJV): "For the Lord God will help me. Therefore, I will not be disgraced; Therefore, I have set My face like a flint, and I know that I will not be ashamed."

Why do we trust in God? Because we know HIM.

Hebrews 4:1-5 (NJKV): "Therefore, since a promise remains of entering His rest, let us fear lest any of you seem to have come short of it. ² For indeed the gospel was preached to us as well as to them; but the word which they heard did not profit them, not being mixed with faith in those who heard *it*. ³ *For we who have believed do enter that rest, as He has said: "So I swore in My wrath, 'They shall not enter My rest, although the works were finished from the foundation of the world*. ⁴ For He has spoken in a certain place of the seventh *day* in this way: "And God rested on the seventh day from all His works"; ⁵ and again in this *place:* "They shall not enter My rest."

At one time in my life, I was so hungry for God I was doing so much in the church because I was overzealous. The Lord gave me this song. "Jesus has done it, think not there's anything you can do. He's won the victory and he's given it straight to you. I receive it. I believe it. He's given it straight to me!"

Jesus finished the work God gave him to do. Now we must go forth and finish the work God has given us to do. We must press toward the mark for the prize of the high calling of God in Christ Jesus.

I have another powerful testimony, where the Word of the Lord prevailed. My sister was hoping that her son and her son's Father would get to know each other. We were confident that God could do it. We were standing on God's Word, in Malachi 4:6 (NJKV): "And he will turn the hearts of the fathers to the children, and the hearts of the children to their fathers, lest I come and strike the earth with a curse."

Today I can report that after 21 years, they have reconciled to each other. When Daniel prayed, it took 21 days for him to get his answer but for us, it took 21 years. We inherit the promises of God through faith and patience. SSSSSSSH! The Word of the Lord prevailed.

I am reminded of another time when the Word of the Lord prevailed. Many years ago, the Lord gave me a word in a dream. The Lord said, "Call George, who was my sister Joyce's husband, and tell him that Michael is going to be okay." I called George and he was reluctant to talk to me, but I was insistent to obey the Lord. With Joyce's encouragement, she convinced him to speak to me. I asked him if he knew someone named Michael and he could not think of anyone. I told him that the Lord told me to tell him that Michael would be okay. I said the Lord said it three times!

Later, George found himself in the hospital where his grandson, Benjamin Michael was experiencing intestinal blockage. The family was very upset and they needed to hear a Word from the Lord.

Since the child was called Benjamin, George did not remember that his middle name was Michael until then. All of a sudden, George spoke in a loud voice saying The Lord said, "Benjamin Michael is going to be OKAY!" He realized that God had already given His Word to him. Everyone believed in the Word of the Lord and stood in faith. Michael is still doing well to this day. God will show you things to prepare you for what is ahead. The Word of the Lord shall prevail!

Father, this is my prayer for the person who is reading this book right now.

Ephesians 1:15-17 (NKJV) Paul said: "Therefore I also, after I heard of your faith in the Lord Jesus and your love for all the saints, do not cease to give thanks for you, making mention of you in my prayers: that the God of our Lord Jesus Christ, the Father of glory, may give to you the spirit of wisdom and revelation in the knowledge of Him, "

How do we apply this to our lives? We make a decision to know our Heavenly Father through His Word. Then, we can confidently say, SSSSSSSH! The Word of the Lord shall prevail.

1 Corinthians 1:30-31 (AMP): "But it is from Him that you have your life in Christ Jesus, Whom God made our Wisdom from God, [revealed to us a knowledge of the divine plan of salvation previously hidden, manifesting itself as] our Righteousness [thus making us upright and putting us in right standing with God], and our

Consecration [making us pure and holy], and our Redemption [providing our ransom from eternal penalty for sin]. So then, as it is written, Let him who boasts and proudly rejoices and glories, boast and proudly rejoice and glory in the LORD."

No matter what comes our way, we believe that God is good and God is love. We believe God is trustworthy. We put our trust in the Lord. We run to God. We run to the Word of God.

Titus 2:11-14 (KJV) *"For the grace of God that bringeth salvation has appeared to all men teaching them that denying ungodliness and worldly lusts that we should live soberly, righteously, and godly in this present world, looking for the blessed hope and glorious appearing of our great God and our savior Jesus Christ."*

CHAPTER 2

SSSSSSSH!
The Word of the Lord Shall Prevail

Heavenly Father, we come to You in the mighty name of Jesus. Holy Spirit, You are welcome in this place. Holy Spirit, You are our teacher, You are our comforter. Lord, flow through me as I teach your Word. Thank you, Father, that your Word always wins and will always prevail in our lives in Jesus Name, Amen.

In the first chapter, I shared examples where the Word of the Lord prevailed in my own life and in the life of others. I want to share examples from the Bible where the Word of the Lord prevailed. I shared how I overcame a great trial of affliction by saying to myself, "SSSSSSSH! Shut up, Betty Jean." Once I quieted my mind, I began to say what the Word of God said concerning the onslaught of fear and sickness from the enemy.

I stated that the reason we can boldly and confidently say that the Word of the Lord shall prevail is because we know God. We put our trust in Christ alone. We glory in the power of the cross. I sing this song to the Lord. Lord to know, know, know you is to love, love, love you. Just to see you smile, makes my life worthwhile. To know, know, know you is to love, love, love you and I do. Yes I do. Yes I do. We know God and we know His Word is true.

Years ago when the Lord showed me how important the Bible is, he put a deep desire in me to share the Word. One day when my Dad was visiting me, I told him that I was so glad to be from his family tree. He looked at me very seriously and said, "Betty, that is good but that is not the most important thing." He said, "The most important thing is that someone would carry on the Word of God in this family and I know that you will, as well as your sister Debi." I know Dad is rejoicing in heaven because now all his offspring are carrying on the Word of God.

Our theme scripture for this book is found in Hebrews 4:12 (KJV): "For the Word of God is quick, and powerful, and sharper than any two-edged sword, piercing even to the dividing asunder of soul and spirit, and of the joints and marrow, and is a discerner of the thoughts and intents of the heart." This is truly the blessing of God, His Holy Word.

What do we do while we are waiting for the Word of the Lord to prevail in our lives and in the lives of others? What do we do until what we are believing for comes to fruition? We keep out mouths shut and we wait on the Lord. Psalm 27:14 (NKJV) "Wait on the Lord; Be of good courage, And He shall strengthen your heart; Wait, I say, on the Lord!" Isaiah 25:9 (NKJV): "And it will be said in that day: "Behold, this is our God; We have waited for Him, and He will save us. This is the Lord; We have waited for Him; We will be glad and rejoice in His salvation." When we hold fast and stand firm, we shall see the Word of the Lord prevail in our lives.

Waiting on the Lord

Also, we must remember not to get side-tracked. There was a time in my life when I was believing for some specific thing to happen. However, I did not stay focused on what I wanted. I kept saying contrary things that did not line up with the vision. I heard the still small voice in my spirit say, "Betty, what do you really want?" I could not even answer. I was stunned. I realized if I didn't know what I wanted, how in the world would God be able to answer me? Isaiah 50:7 (NKJV) "For the Lord God will help Me; therefore I will not be disgraced; Therefore I have set My face like a flint. And I know that I will not be ashamed." Ezekiel 3:8-9 (NKJV) "Behold, I have made your face strong against their faces, and your forehead strong against their foreheads. Like adamant stone, harder than flint, I have made your forehead; do not be afraid of them, nor be dismayed at their looks, though they are a rebellious house." We must stay focused and look to Jesus!

What else can we do until our answer comes? Just know that all the promises of God are Yes and Amen! God is for you and not against you. God has great plans for you. God loves you and God wants you to fulfill your destiny. You follow Ephesians 5:19-20 (NKJV): "Speaking to one another in psalms and hymns and spiritual songs, singing and making melody in your heart to the Lord, giving thanks always for all things to God the Father in the name of our Lord Jesus Christ."

The first example I want to share comes from Joshua Chapter 6:1-10 (NJKV): "Now Jericho was securely shut up because of the children of Israel; none went out, and none came in.² And the LORD said to Joshua: "See! I have given Jericho into your hand, its king, *and* the mighty men of valor. ³ You shall march around the city, all *you* men of war; you shall go all around the city once. This you shall do six days. ⁴ And seven priests shall bear seven trumpets of rams' horns before the ark. But the seventh day you shall march around the city seven times, and the priests

24

shall blow the trumpets. ⁵ It shall come to pass, when they make a long *blast* with the ram's horn, *and* when you hear the sound of the trumpet, that all the people shall shout with a great shout; then the wall of the city will fall down flat. And the people shall go up every man straight before him." ⁶ Then Joshua the son of Nun called the priests and said to them, "Take up the ark of the covenant, and let seven priests bear seven trumpets of rams' horns before the ark of the LORD." ⁷ And he said to the people, "Proceed, and march around the city, and let him who is armed advance before the ark of the LORD." ⁸ So it was, when Joshua had spoken to the people, that the seven priests bearing the seven trumpets of rams' horns before the LORD advanced and blew the trumpets, and the ark of the covenant of the LORD followed them. ⁹ The armed men went before the priests who blew the trumpets, and the rear guard came after the ark, while *the priests* continued blowing the trumpets. ¹⁰ Now Joshua had commanded the people, saying, "You shall not shout or make any noise with your voice, nor shall a word proceed out of your mouth, until the day I say to you, 'Shout!' Then you shall shout." In other words, Shut up, be quiet and when I tell you to shout, you will shout!

God desires that we fully believe that He is true to His promises, even before they are manifested in the physical realm. There are three degrees of faith here:

1. The faith that rested on the truth of God's Word.
2. The faith that reckoned God would do it.
3. The faith that reached – it dared to march around the walls.

God gave them very specific instructions. They obeyed every word God said to them. Our responsibility for our situations is to do the same. We are to ask God, believe God, receive the answer by faith and follow God's instructions. If God says, be still and see my salvation, then we need to be still. When God says go, we need to go. When God says stop, we need to stop.

The Israelites were required to follow unusual, yet explicit instructions, which would test their obedience and their faith in God. In faith, as they fulfilled the final instruction, the walls of Jericho fell down. Rahab and her family had been spared because Rahab was a woman of faith. Her faith brought action and saved her family. The scarlet cord in Rahab's window became her cord of deliverance. It was symbolic of the blood of

Jesus. She became a wife of a Prince in Judah, the mother of Boaz, one of David's grandmothers, and one of the Savior's ancestors.

The Israelites were never to give up. They were to follow God's leading joyfully and await patiently the manifestation of victory. We also are to be of good cheer, as we await the manifestation of our victory. Jesus has overcome and we are in Him. Follow God's leading and possess your possessions. Joshua teaches us how to possess our inheritance. They had to enter in and we also must enter in and possess our inheritance, which is the mighty promise of God through Christ Jesus our Lord.

Now, I will share about a time when the Word of the Lord prevailed and it is found in 2 Kings 4:8-37 (NKJV): "Now it happened one day that Elisha went to Shunem, where there *was* a notable woman, and she persuaded him to eat some food. So it was, as often as he passed by, he would turn in there to eat some food. And she said to her husband, "Look now, I know that this *is* a holy man of God, who passes by us regularly. Please, let us make a small upper room on the wall; and let us put a bed for him there, and a table and a chair and a lampstand; so it will be, whenever he comes to us, he can turn in there." And it happened one day that he came there, and he turned in to the upper room and lay down there. Then he said to Gehazi his servant, "Call this Shunammite woman." When he had called her, she stood before him. And he said to him, "Say now to her, 'Look, you have been concerned for us with all this care. What *can I* do for you? Do you want me to speak on your behalf to the king or to the commander of the army?' She answered, "I dwell among my own people." So he said, "What then *is* to be done for her?" And Gehazi answered, "Actually, she has no son, and her husband is old." So he said, "Call her." When he had called her, she stood in the doorway. ¹⁶ Then he said, "About this time next year you shall embrace a son." And she said, "No, my lord. Man of God, do not lie to your maidservant!" ¹⁷ But the woman conceived, and bore a son when the appointed time had come, of which Elisha had told her. ¹⁸ And the child grew. Now it happened one day that he went out to his father, to the reapers. ¹⁹ And he said to his father, "My head, my head!"

So he said to a servant, "Carry him to his mother." ²⁰ When he had taken him and brought him to his mother, he sat on her knees till noon, and *then* died. ²¹ And she went up and laid him on the bed of the man of God, shut *the door* upon him, and went out. ²² Then she called to her husband, and said, "Please send me one of the young men and one of the donkeys, that I may run to the man of God and come back." ²³ So he said, "Why are you going to him today? *It is* neither the New Moon nor the Sabbath."

And she said, "*It is* well." ²⁴ Then she saddled a donkey, and said to her servant, "Drive, and go forward; do not slacken the pace for me unless I tell you." ²⁵ And so she departed, and went to the man of God at Mount Carmel. So it was, when the man of God saw her afar off, that he said to his servant Gehazi, "Look, the Shunammite woman! ²⁶ Please run now to meet her, and say to her, '*Is it* well with you? *Is it* well with your husband? *Is it* well with the child?'"And she answered, "*It is* well." ²⁷ Now when she came to the man of God at the hill, she caught him by the feet, but Gehazi came near to push her away. But the man of God said, "Let her alone; for her soul *is* in deep distress, and the Lord has hidden *it* from me, and has not told me."²⁸ So she said, "Did I ask a son of my lord? Did I not say, 'Do not deceive me'?"²⁹ Then he said to Gehazi,

"Get yourself ready, and take my staff in your hand, and be on your way. If you meet anyone, do not greet him; and if anyone greets you, do not answer him; but lay my staff on the face of the child."[30] And the mother of the child said, "*As* the LORD lives, and *as* your soul lives, I will not leave you." So he arose and followed her. [31] Now Gehazi went on ahead of them, and laid the staff on the face of the child; but *there was* neither voice nor hearing. Therefore he went back to meet him, and told him, saying, "The child has not awakened." When Elisha came into the house, there was the child, lying dead on his bed. [33] He went in therefore, shut the door behind the two of them, and prayed to the LORD. [34] And he went up and lay on the child, and put his mouth on his mouth, his eyes on his eyes, and his hands on his hands; and he stretched himself out on the child, and the flesh of the child became warm. [35] He returned and walked back and forth in the house, and again went up and stretched himself out on him; then the child sneezed seven times, and the child opened his eyes. [36] And he called Gehazi and said, "Call this Shunammite woman." So he called her. And when she came in to him, he said, "Pick up your son." [37] So she went in, fell at his feet, and bowed to the ground; then she picked up her son and went out."

This is one of my favorite stories in the Bible. First of all, this woman was able to convince her husband to make a room for the man of God. Secondly, by her response to Elisha, she must have really wanted a child but wasn't sure it could happen. The most important part is she was able to keep her mouth shut and all she would say was, "IT IS WELL."

We know from the story that in the natural her son, whom the man of God promised she would have, is now dead. Notice how she gave instruction to the servants. She was very clear and explicit. Notice how she would not leave the man of God. Even though Gehazi had the staff of Elisha, nothing happened. That is why the Bible says, let no man take your crown. God has given you a destiny. God has given you a dream and His Word will prevail in your life. Just praise the Lord, keep the words of your mouth and the meditation of your heart acceptable unto the Lord. That is exactly what the Shunammite woman did. She was pleasing to God. She had faith that if the man of God prayed for her to have a child, he could pray for God to raise him from the dead.

Elisha went up and lay on the child and did mouth to mouth resuscitation and the child became warm. But Elisha had to go back a second time and stretch himself out on the child again. It was then that the child sneezed seven times and opened his eyes. I can only imagine that the first thing she did after she embraced him was to feed him.

We wait patiently for the manifestation of the Word of the Lord to prevail in our lives. A prophet is led by the Holy Spirit. A false prophet is a false prophet. Elisha did not know what problem the Shunammite woman was bringing to him. He told Gehazi that the Lord did not reveal it to him or let him know. A true prophet only speaks what he hears the Lord saying. We must always give glory to God. A prophet carries the gift from God and speaks on God's behalf. Also, remember that the Holy Spirit and the Word must line up together concerning the Word of the Lord.

To me, the most powerful Bible story concerning when the word of the Lord prevailed is the story of Elijah, Found in 1 Kings, Chapter 18.

The prophets of Baal, a false god were trying to prove that their god was the true God. Elijah knew and believed that his God was true. Elijah was serving the God of Abraham, Isaac and

Jacob. When put to the test, Baal did not make an appearance. However, our God showed up and showed off. The fire of the Lord fell and consumed the burnt sacrifice and the wood and the stones and licked up the water that was in the trench. Let us read the account.

1 Kings 18:30-40 (KJV): "And Elijah said unto all the people, Come near unto me. And all the people came near unto him. And he repaired the altar of the LORD that was broken down. And Elijah took twelve stones, according to the number of the tribes of the sons of Jacob, unto whom the word of the LORD came, saying, Israel shall be thy name: And with the stones he built an altar in the name of the LORD: and he made a trench about the altar, as great as would contain two measures of seed. And he put the wood in order, and cut the bullock in pieces, and laid him on the wood, and said, Fill four barrels with water, and pour it on the burnt sacrifice, and on the wood. And he said, Do it the second time. And they did it the second time. And he said, Do it the third time. And they did it the third time. And the water ran round about the altar; and he filled the trench also with water. And it came to pass at the time of the offering of the evening sacrifice, that Elijah the prophet came

near, and said, LORD God of Abraham, Isaac, and of Israel, let it be known this day that thou art God in Israel, and that I am thy servant, and that I have done all these things at thy word. Hear me, O LORD, hear me, that this people may know that thou art the LORD God, and that thou hast turned their heart back again. Then the fire of the LORD fell, and consumed the burnt sacrifice, and the wood, and the stones, and the dust, and licked up the water that was in the trench. And when all the people saw it, they fell on their faces: and they said, The LORD, he is the God; the LORD, he is the God. And Elijah said unto them, Take the prophets of Baal; let not one of them escape. And they took them: and Elijah brought them down to the brook Kishon, and slew them there."

Notice in verse 36 Elijah had done all he did at the Word from God.

The coolest thing or maybe I should say the hottest thing about the Word of God is that when the fire from God comes it burns out the dross in us and brings forth the gold. Jesus increases and we decrease.

In these examples, you can see that they trusted in the Lord. They had the knowledge of God. They had heard from God and they knew that the Word of the Lord would prevail in their lives. The Lord has given me so much concerning this topic that I will be sharing more in our next chapter.

Heavenly Father, in Jesus' name I thank you that your Word will not return to You void, but it shall accomplish what you sent it to do. I thank you that every heart has rich soil for your engrafted Word and that the Word will dwell richly within each one reading this book.

CHAPTER 3

SSSSSSSH!
The Word of the Lord Shall Prevail

Heavenly Father, we pray that you will empower us to mix the Word with faith. Holy Spirit, you are welcome in this place. Holy Spirit, you are our teacher. My tongue is the pen of a ready writer, ready to write the words you desire to speak, in the name of Jesus Christ of Nazareth, Amen.

Let us continue with the message that the Lord gave me. The rest of my life, I will be sharing how important the Word of God is to our lives. Now I know why my Dad said that the most important thing one could do is to carry on the gospel of Jesus Christ. I am so glad that God called me, God anointed me, and God ordained me to teach the Word. Glory to God!

I will give an example of Jehoshaphat seeking God, knowing God's plan for his life and the life of the whole nation. We will see how Jehoshaphat did everything God said to do. We will share an example of the Word of the Lord prevailing in my husband's life and one in my own life. Why can we boldly and confidently say the Word of the Lord shall prevail? We can say that because we have the knowledge of God, and we believe what the Holy Bible says. We trust in our Heavenly Father that His Word will accomplish exactly what He sends it to accomplish. We say that because we stand alone on the Word of the Lord.

Hebrews 4:2 (NKJV) "For indeed the gospel was preached to us as well as to them; but the word which they heard did not profit them, not being mixed with faith in those who heard it."

We know that without faith, it is impossible to please God. Therefore, since we all have been given the measure of faith, we can all believe and have faith toward God as we hear the Word.

The first example we want to share is found in 2 Chronicles, Chapter 20. First Jehoshaphat feared, then he inquired of the Lord, then there was praying, fasting, worshipping and praising. As we look at this story, we can learn how to become someone who inquires of the Lord, then prays, someone who fasts, and someone who obeys the Word of the Lord and someone who praises.

I would see my Dad pray, fast and praise and I wanted to be just like him. In high school, I would pray and fast, but I did not know this story or how important it was to praise even though I saw my Dad do it continually. Anytime he had a flat tire, he would get out of the car and begin rejoicing and praising God as he set about his task of changing the tire. When he would almost run out of gas on the way home from preaching, he would start praising God and thanking him for supernaturally getting us home on the empty tank. We were never stranded on the road because we had run out of gas.

We would be in the car with Dad and the traffic light would turn red. Dad would start clapping and singing and praising God. Then we would pull out and he was so happy praising the Lord that he would take his hands off the steering wheel and start clapping and praising some more. We would yell, "Dad, put your hands on the steering wheel." Of course, he was using his legs to steer; we just didn't know until we were older. You see God was always the pilot of Dad's ship. God was always steering his path. I have good news. God can be the pilot of your ship if you will let him have the reins in your life and you surrender your life to him.

Since then, God has shown me that actually I am the captain of my own ship. He is my Master, my Savior, my healer, and the captain of my salvation.

Let us get back to Jehoshaphat. Jehoshaphat was the king of Jerusalem when the children of Judah all worshipped the Lord. Judah was a very wealthy kingdom and the children were well fed because Jehoshaphat studied and obeyed the Word of the Lord.

Then Jehoshaphat received a bad report. Sounds familiar, we are doing well and then we get a bad report. Well, what are we supposed to do? Let us continue to look at the story and follow their example.

Well, out of the east came an army after Jehoshaphat's gold. They told Jehoshaphat right away. He called all the people together. They chose to fast and pray. The Lord told all the people that there was no need to be afraid. The Bible said that he feared when he got the bad report. However, he did not camp out there. He immediately sought the Lord to get the Word of the Lord. Once we rebuke fear and cast it out, then we need to seek the Lord and inquire of the Lord.

2 Chronicles 20:5-12 (NKJV): "Then Jehoshaphat stood in the assembly of Judah and Jerusalem, in the house of the Lord, before the new

39

court and said, "O Lord God of our fathers, are You not God in heaven, and do You not rule over all the kingdoms of the nations, and in Your hand is there not power and might, so that no one is able to withstand You? Are You not our God, who drove out the inhabitants of this land before Your people Israel, and gave it to the descendants of Abraham Your friend forever? And they dwell in it, and have built You a sanctuary in it for Your name, saying. If disaster comes upon us—sword, judgment, pestilence, or famine—we will stand before this temple and in Your presence (for Your name is in this temple), and cry out to You in our affliction, and You will hear and save. And now, here are the people of Ammon, Moab, and Mount Seir—whom You would not let Israel invade when they came out of the land of Egypt, but they turned from them and did not destroy them—here they are, rewarding us by coming to throw us out of Your possession which you have given us to inherit. O our God, will You not judge them? For we have no power against this great multitude that is coming against us; nor do we know what to do, but our eyes are upon YOU."

A golden key for us is that we would focus on God and keep our eyes upon HIM. We know that God lives in the praises of His people. Therefore, if you want the presence of God in your life, become a person of praise!

Then, as you know the story, the Spirit of the Lord came upon Jahaziel and he let them know that God said that they were not to be afraid because the battle was God's, not theirs. What a relief! If we could camp out there and have the knowledge of God to such a capacity that we could let go and let God! I want to grow to that place. I am headed there now in the name of Jesus.

As you read this story, you can see that God gave them specific instructions and they obeyed. Isn't it interesting that Jehoshaphat chose some singers and they were to sing and praise the beauty of holiness instead of shouting out a battle cry. Notice, that it was WHEN they began to sing and to praise, the Lord set ambushes against the people of Ammon, Moab, and Mount Seir, who had come against Judah. They were defeated.

2 Chronicles 20:25-30 (NKJV): "When Jehoshaphat and his people came to take away their spoil, they found among them an abundance of valuables on the dead bodies, and precious jewelry, which they stripped off for themselves, more than they could carry away; and they were three days gathering the spoil because there was so much. And on the fourth day they assembled in the Valley of Berachah, for there they blessed the LORD; therefore the name of that place was

41

called The Valley of Berachah until this day. Then they returned, every man of Judah and Jerusalem, with Jehoshaphat in front of them, to go back to Jerusalem with joy, for the LORD had made them rejoice over their enemies. So they came to Jerusalem, with stringed instruments and harps and trumpets, to the house of the LORD. And the fear of God was on all the kingdoms of *those* countries when they heard that the LORD had fought against the enemies of Israel. Then the realm of Jehoshaphat was quiet, for his God gave him rest all around."

When you get a bad report, believe in your Heavenly Father and believe that His word is true. Start praising and worshipping and inquire of the Lord. We will believe the report of the Lord. His report says that we are healed; His report says VICTORY!

Healing There was a time when my husband Rusty and I stood on God's Word in 1 Peter 2:24 and Isaiah 53:5 concerning healing. By the stripes of Jesus we are healed and by the stripes of Jesus we were healed. It is the past tense and present tense. We were healed and we are presently healed.

Rusty was playing softball and sprained his ankle, as he had done many times before. After several weeks of feeling unusual pain in his calf and going to his normal doctor, he decided to go to a specialist. The specialist discovered that Rusty had a blood clot in his ankle. Because of a missed diagnosis by his primary physician, the problem could not be resolved by medicine or surgery. The doctor told him he would lose his leg somewhere below his knee.

After several weeks of ischemia pain, (caused by lack of oxygen to the flesh and gangrene in his toes), someone suggested he see a particular herbologist. After trying her remedy, which included soaking in a hot mixture for several weeks, blood flow began to slowly increase in his toes, reversing the gangrene. At that time, his surgeon became encouraged to the point that he told Rusty, "If we can save your heel, it will make it easier to give you an artificial foot. That is when Rusty told the doctor in anger, "The only thing I might lose is a toenail." Looking back Rusty said, "It is true death and life are in the power of the tongue." He wished he had believed that he would not lose his toenail.

After several months of the slow healing process, he only lost a toenail. The whole ordeal lasted fifteen months with open wounds on his leg.

During this time, our nurse friend would come by and help clean and medicate the wound. Now he can play ball and he completely recovered.

God is good! The Word of the Lord prevailed in Rusty's life. Hallelujah!! We surely had to let go of the bad report and let God perform his miraculous work. Nothing is too hard for God! All we can continue to do is praise God and thank God for his great love and healing. God is love and God loves you and me. <u>God heals and God heals you and me.</u>

How many of you have ever been through a wilderness? I personally always hoped that I would not have to go through a wilderness experience. However, in my life I have had to walk through some valleys and it was hard. I knew there was only one set of footprints in my life going through every wilderness. Somehow in my spirit I knew Jesus was carrying me. There is a light at the end of the tunnel. I know the Lord will carry you through any valley you go through. The Lord will be with us always even unto the end of the world.

1978 began as a terrible year in my life but ended gloriously. That was the year that I went through a divorce because my husband committed adultery against God and me. He found someone else he wanted to be with and share his life. Almost every year prior to this, he would threaten to divorce me. Finally in 1978, I heard a Word from the Lord. The Word was, "God will not be late in 78." I grabbed that word like a dog grabs a bone and I would not let go. I knew that God was going to deliver me from a terrible marriage. In 1978, my ex-husband said, "I want a divorce, I want to be free." I said I would agree only if he would agree for me to have custody of our sons. We went to our attorney together. It was highly recommended that we file in my name because the judge would find it favorable because I had custody of the children. We took his recommendation. I knew God would forgive me because my ex-husband had committed adultery against me. The Bible also says if a man is not pleased to dwell with you then let him depart. He was not happy to live with me and so he departed. My Dad had taught me that a person could not have a divorce except for adultery. My Dad knew how sad I was about this situation. When I spoke over the telephone with him, he assured me that I would be free to re-marry because my ex-husband had committed adultery. Dad assured me that God still loved me and God would take care of me.

Just before my sons and I moved into our condo, I was standing in our kitchen and the Word of the Lord came to me. I heard the voice of the Lord as clearly as you hear a bell. He said, "I will take care of you; I will take care of John; I will take care of Jeff."

Nevertheless, the pain was still excruciating. I found the scriptures to comfort my heart through this time of being rejected by a man. Isaiah 54:6-7 (KJV): "For the Lord hath called thee as a woman forsaken and grieved in spirit, and a wife of youth, when thou wast refused, saith thy God. For a small moment have I forsaken thee, but with great mercies will I gather thee." I had definitely been refused and rejected. However, I stood on this scripture that God would have mercy on me. I spent many years so discouraged and after meditating on this particular scripture, I knew everything concerning me would be healed.

Another scripture that was my mainstay during this troubling time is found in Isaiah 35:4-10 (KJV): "Say to them that are of a fearful heart, Be strong, fear not: behold, your God will come with vengeance, even God with a recompense; he will come and save you. Then the eyes of the blind shall be opened, and the ears of the deaf shall be unstopped. Then shall the lame man leap as an hart, and the tongue of the dumb sing: for in the wilderness shall waters break out, and streams in the desert. And the parched ground shall become a pool, and the thirsty land springs of water: in the habitation of dragons, where each lay, shall be grass with reeds and rushes. And an highway shall be there, and a way, and it shall be called The way of holiness; the unclean shall not pass over it; but it shall be for those: the wayfaring men, though fools, shall not err therein. No lion shall be there, nor any ravenous beast shall go up thereon, it shall not be found there; but the redeemed shall walk there: And the ransomed of the LORD shall return, and come to Zion with songs and everlasting joy upon their heads: they shall obtain joy and gladness, and sorrow and sighing shall flee away."

I attended a Bible study and a man of God had a word from the Lord for me. He said, "You are in a wilderness now, but God says he is going to bring rivers in your wilderness and streams in your desert." That was a very encouraging word so this is where I found the word in the Scripture. If you get a word from the Lord through anyone, make sure it lines up with God's Word, because the Holy Spirit and the Word always agree.

I shared that the end of 1978 was glorious. My divorce was in September and in October of 1978 my sons asked Jesus to come into their hearts. The happiest days of my life were when my sons were born. The most glorious days of my life were when my sons invited Jesus into their hearts and they were **born again** into the kingdom of God. We had recently moved into a condo at Paradise Beach Condominiums. They had gotten into a little mischief and we were talking about it upstairs in my bedroom. I prayed for them and said, "Boys, what you really need is to ask Jesus to come into your hearts." I shared the plan of salvation with them and they both accepted Jesus into their hearts. I was so happy that day. Even in the midst of all the rejection that I was experiencing, John and Jeff's salvation made my 1978 the most glorious of all. I knew the angels were rejoicing in heaven that John and Jeff had come home to Jesus.

When you are facing any difficult situation, search diligently for what God says about your situation. Let that Word grow and develop in every fiber of your being. Let the Word of God rule in your heart and the peace of God which passes all understanding will guard your heart and mind in Christ Jesus. Always run to God first. He is our Abba Father and he loves us so much!

Heavenly Father, I thank you that your Word will not return unto you void but it will accomplish what you sent it for now in Jesus' name. Thank you for the story of Jehoshaphat. Thank you for bringing my sons into a saving knowledge of Jesus Christ and for healing my husband, Rusty. You are an awesome God, and we praise You and worship You. Thank you for your great love. You gave your only begotten Son that whosoever believeth in him should not perish but have everlasting life. Thank you for my precious life. I do not take it for granted. Thank you, God, that you are a present help in the time of trouble.

Father, from this day forward, I choose to run to you anytime I get a bad report. I choose to pray and fast and seek your face and wait to hear from you for your report. Lord, I choose to believe Your report, above every bad report, in Jesus name, Amen.

Chapter 4

SSSSSSSH!
Knowing God's Glorious Grace

Father in the name of Jesus, we thank you for the opportunity to minister your Word concerning your great grace. My tongue is the pen of a ready writer ready to speak your Word. Holy Spirit, you are welcome in this place. Thank you for being our teacher, our comforter and our guide. Be glorified, Father, in Jesus' name, Amen.

The reason we can confidently and boldly say to ourselves, "SSSSSSSH! The Word of the Lord shall prevail is because we KNOW GOD! To know God is to be knowledgeable of His Word. We will remind ourselves of knowing God in His great grace.

I.   What is Grace?

Simply put, grace can be defined as God's unmerited favor. It is God's free action for the benefit of His people. God's grace can be compared to a pardon that is given to a guilty criminal, who is facing execution because of his/her crime. Without this pardon, without this grace, they will be given what they deserve.

Grace is getting what we do not deserve. Justice is getting what we deserve. Mercy is not getting what we deserve. Grace reigns through righteousness. Grace is also known as God's riches at Christ's expense. Jesus paid it all. However, God so loved us that he GAVE His only begotten Son.

Romans 5:18-21 (NKJV) "Therefore, as through one man's offense judgment came to all men, resulting in condemnation even so through one man's righteous act the free gift came to all men, resulting in justification of life. For as by one man's disobedience many were made sinners, so also by one Man's obedience many will be made righteous. Moreover the law entered that the offense might abound. But where sin abounded, grace abounded much more, so that as sin reigned in death even so grace might reign through righteousness to eternal life through Jesus Christ our Lord."

Philippians 2:8-11 (NKJV) "And being found in appearance as a man, He humbled Himself and became obedient to the point of death, even the death of the cross. Therefore God also has highly exalted Him and given Him the name which is above every name, that at the name of Jesus every knee should bow, of those in heaven, and of those on earth, and of those under the earth and that every tongue should confess that Jesus Christ is Lord, to the glory of God the Father."

Did you know that every time we confess that Jesus Christ is Lord, it brings glory to our Heavenly Father?

Grace is the power of God to do for us what we could not do for ourselves. Jesus says in John 15:5 (NKJV): "I am the vine, you are the branches, He who abides in Me and I in him, bears much fruit, for without Me you can do nothing."

It is the precious work of Calvary that brought us grace. Jesus took upon Him the nature of man and established His cross between earth and heaven. Through the cross, man was drawn to God and God to man. Titus 2:11 (KJV): "For the grace of God that bringeth salvation has appeared to all men." God has shown us all His grace through the power of the cross. The Bible says that God's grace has appeared to all men. Some people have said that it is grace alone that has saved us. However, we had to exercise faith to receive the grace of God and his completed work at

Calvary. Faith takes hold of Christ in love. Faith works by love. However, we know that man's role is miniscule in view of God's marvelous grace and all glory belongs to God.

II. What has grace given to us including salvation?

We are saved by grace. Ephesians 2:5
We are called by grace. Jeremiah 1:4-5
The heart is established by grace.
Hebrews 13:9
We are justified by grace. Titus 3:7
Grace imparts everlasting consolation.
2 Thess. 2:16

III. What do we do with this grace?

We are NOT to receive the grace of God in vain.

With this grace we are to:
> Live soberly.
> Live righteously.
> Live godly in this present world.
> We are to look for the blessed hope and glorious appearing of our great God and our Savior Jesus Christ.

Even though God has bestowed his grace upon us, we still have a desire to grow in the knowledge of Jesus, in the knowledge of the Word and to KNOW God in a more intimate way. Romans 6:1-2 (NKJV): "What shall we say then? Shall we continue in sin that grace may abound? Certainly not! How shall we who died to sin live any longer in it?" Then Romans 6:6-7 (NKJV): "Knowing this that our old man was crucified with Him that the body of sin might be done away with, that we should no longer be slaves of sin. For he who has died has been freed from sin."

Galatians 2:20 (NKJV) "I have been crucified with Christ; it is no longer I who live, but Christ lives in me; and the life which I now live in the flesh I live by faith in the Son of God, who loved me and gave himself for me."

IV. What are two examples of people who found favor/grace with God?

The first one is in the book of Ruth. I have often prayed, "Lord give me the heart of Ruth full of faithfulness and truth." We know that she followed Naomi because she knew Naomi's God was true.

This story may be similar to many of people's lives today. Maybe you are not in the best situation. Maybe you have lost a loved one. Maybe you are not filled with the joy of the Lord when you wake up every morning. I have good news for you. The Word of the Lord will prevail in your life. Keep your mind free of bad thoughts and focus on the Word, focus on what God has in store for you. According to Jeremiah 29:11, God has great plans for you and none of them include defeat.

The beginning of the book of Ruth is very sad. There was a famine in the land and her husband , Elimelech, took Ruth and their two sons and moved to Moab. Ruth's husband and two sons had died. Her sons had two wives left, Orpah and Ruth. Naomi encouraged both of her daughter-in-laws to go back to their own homes. Orpah kissed Naomi and went back to her mother's house, but Ruth would not leave. Ruth trusted Naomi and insisted on staying.

Ruth went back to Bethlehem with Naomi. Let us read the words that Naomi and Ruth spoke to each other.

Ruth 1:15-18 King James Version (KJV): "And she said, Behold, thy sister in law is gone back unto her people, and unto her gods: return thou after thy sister in law. And Ruth said, Intreat me not to leave thee, or to return from following after thee: for whither thou goest, I will go; and where thou lodgest, I will lodge: thy people shall be my people, and thy God my God: Where thou diest, will I die, and there will I be buried: the LORD do so to me, and more also, if ought but death part thee and me. When she saw that she was steadfastly minded to go with her, then she left speaking unto her."

Naomi and Ruth went back to Bethlehem. The people were really excited. She must have been a well-known woman. Let us read about it.

Ruth 1:19-22 King James Version (KJV): "So they two went until they came to Bethlehem. And it came to pass, when they were come to Bethlehem, that all the city was moved about them, and they said, Is this Naomi? And she said unto them, Call me not Naomi, call me Mara: for the Almighty hath dealt very bitterly with me. I went out full and the LORD hath brought me home again empty: why then call ye me Naomi, seeing the LORD hath testified against me, and the Almighty hath afflicted me? So Naomi returned, and Ruth the Moabitess, her daughter in law, with her, which returned out of the country of Moab: and they came to Bethlehem in the beginning of barley harvest."

Naomi was full of sorrow when she returned. God gives us gladness for mourning and peace for despair.

Boaz was a relative of Naomi's husband and he was very wealthy. Knowing this, Ruth asked Naomi if she could glean in Boaz's barley field. Right away, Boaz protected Ruth and gave her grace. Let us read the story:

Ruth 2:8-13King James Version (KJV): "Then said Boaz unto Ruth, Hearest thou not, my daughter? Go not to glean in another field, neither go from hence, but abide here fast by my maidens: Let thine eyes be on the field that they do reap, and go thou after them: have I not charged the young men that they shall not touch thee? and when thou art athirst, go unto the vessels, and drink of that which the young men have drawn. Then she fell on her face, and bowed herself to the ground, and said unto him, Why have I found grace in thine eyes, that thou shouldest take knowledge of me, seeing I am a stranger? And Boaz answered and said unto her, It hath fully been shewed me, all that thou hast done unto thy mother in law since the death of thine husband: and how thou hast left thy father and thy mother, and the land of thy nativity, and art come unto a people which thou knewest not heretofore. The LORD recompense thy work, and a full reward be given thee of the LORD God of Israel, under whose wings thou art come to trust. Then she said, Let me find favour in thy sight, my lord; for that thou hast comforted me, and for that thou hast spoken friendly unto thine handmaid, though I be not like unto one of thine handmaidens."

Notice that even later after Boaz told Ruth she had found favor that she asked him again for favor and she praised him for comforting her and speaking kindly to her even though she was a foreigner.

We also must continue not only just to receive God's grace, but to continue to grow in grace and favor. 2 Peter 3:18 (NKJV): "But grow in the grace and knowledge of our Lord and Savior Jesus Christ. To Him be the glory both now and forever. Amen."

Do you realize that when Ruth decided to follow Naomi's God, she made an excellent choice. Next, she chose to follow Naomi because of the God of Israel. In this situation, Ruth found favor/grace because she was connected with Naomi, whom Boaz highly respected and he was a kinsman redeemer. Ruth waited for her Boaz. Boaz chose to marry Ruth. By God's grace, stay connected with the people of God. This is very true in my life. Because they knew my sister, I was hired at my first job at the state capital in West Virginia.

Praise God that Naomi's mourning ended when Ruth gave birth to Obed. Then Naomi took the child and laid him on her bosom and became a nurse to him. The neighbor woman gave him a name saying, "There is a son born to Naomi." And they called his name Obed. He is the father of Jesse, the father of David. Ruth 4:22 (NKJV): "Obed begot Jesse, and Jesse begot David."

David was a man after God's own heart. There is joy when we continually follow the Word of the Lord. Naomi was very sad but I'm confident there were times when she had to quiet her mind and say, SSSSSSSH! The Lord God of Israel will heal my heart. God did much more than that, he gave her Obed to nurse and bring life to her! To me, a newborn baby is the greatest gift God can give us.

Noah is another example in the Bible of someone who found favor/grace with God.

Genesis 6:5-8 (NKJV): "When the LORD saw that the wickedness of man *was* great in the earth, and *that* every intent of the thoughts of his heart *was* only evil continually. And the LORD was sorry that He had made man on the earth, and He was grieved in His heart. So the LORD said, "I will destroy man whom I have created from the face of the earth, both man and beast, creeping thing and birds of the air, for I am sorry that I have made them." But Noah found grace in the eyes of the LORD."

Psalm 84:11 (NKJV): "For the Lord God is a sun and shield; The Lord will give grace and glory, No good thing will He withhold from those who walk uprightly."

Isaiah 60:19-20 (NKJV): "The sun shall no longer be your light by day. Nor for brightness shall the moon give light to you; But the Lord will be to you an everlasting light, and your God your glory. Your sun shall no longer go down. Nor shall your moon withdraw itself; For the Lord will be your everlasting light, and the days of your mourning shall be ended. "

If Noah had not found grace in the sight of the Lord, we would not be here today. Praise God that Noah found grace in the eyes of the Lord and he landed high and dry. We know the story of Noah. It is a beautiful story and the ending is the most beautiful of all.

Genesis 9:8-17 (NKJV): "Then God spoke to Noah and to his sons with him saying: "And as for Me, behold, I establish My covenant with you and with your descendants after you. and with every living creature that is with you: the birds, the cattle, and every beast of the earth with you of all that go out of the ark, every beast of the earth. Thus I establish my covenant with you: Never again shall all flesh be cut off by the waters of the flood; never again shall there be a flood to destroy the earth. And God said, This is the sign of the covenant which I make between Me and you, and every living creature that is with you, for perpetual generations: I set My rainbow in the cloud, and it shall be for the sign of the covenant between Me and the earth. It shall be, when I bring a cloud over the earth, that the rainbow shall be seen in the cloud; and I will remember My covenant which is between Me and you and every living creature of all flesh; the waters shall NEVER again become a flood to destroy all flesh. "The rainbow shall be in the cloud, and I will look on it to remember the everlasting covenant between God and every living creature of all flesh that is on the earth. And God said to Noah, "This is the sign of the covenant which I have established between Me and all the flesh that is on the earth."

Just imagine how many times Noah probably had to say to himself, "SSSSSSSH! The Word of the Lord Shall Prevail." Who knows how much criticism Noah had to endure. I wonder how many people made fun of him when he started building the ark. But, Praise God the Word of the Lord prevailed with Noah. Noah obeyed the precise instructions of the Lord. We are to go and do likewise. We are to obey God and His Word. If God says it, believe and walk in faith in God.

We can boldly and confidently say, SSSSSSSH! The Word of the Lord Shall Prevail, because we know God. We know how he spoke in the Old Testament as well as the New Testament. We know that every word was written by men inspired by God, the Father, Son and Holy Spirit.

We have heard an example of Ruth, who not only obtained grace from Boaz but asked that she would continue to find favor in his eyes. We saw God ready to destroy all mankind until he found

Noah, who found grace in God's eyes. We must pray for America that men will be saved and walk in obedience to God's commandments. The next time we see God's rainbow in the sky, let's praise and thank God that His grace has been extended to all mankind.

Father, I thank you that your Word will not return unto you void, but will accomplish what you sent it to accomplish. We praise you for your powerful Word to our hearts.

Say this after me:
Lord, we need your grace and mercy
Lord, your word shall prevail
Lord, we long to know you and the width, depth, length and height of your love toward us.
Truly Lord, your grace is amazing.

In the name of Jesus Christ of Nazareth, Amen.

CHAPTER 5

SSSSSSSH!

Knowing God in Our

Blessed Redemption

Heavenly Father, we come to you in the mighty and matchless name of Jesus. Let the words of my mouth and the meditations of my heart be acceptable in thy sight, Oh Lord, my strength and my redeemer. My tongue is the pen of a ready writer ready to speak those words you have placed in my heart. May I only say things that will be pleasing to you, Our Father in heaven. We give you all the honor, all the glory and all the praise that Your Word shall go forth unhindered. Be glorified, Oh Father, we pray in Jesus' name. Amen

When we come to Christ, we receive the new birth. When we receive the new birth, all of heaven's blessings are opened to us. As we know,

God has given us everything that pertains to LIFE and Godliness. We have been redeemed at Calvary.

Let us look at the definition of redeem. Redeem means to recover ownership of by paying a specified sum: To pay off. To set free; rescue, to save from sin and its consequences. Redeemer is a person who redeems; a savior, Jesus Christ. Redemption is the act of redeeming or the condition of being redeemed.

Therefore, we can say, Christ, our Savior has paid a specified sum to set us free and to save us from sin and its consequences. Through Christ, I have been redeemed. Through Christ, you have been redeemed.

The specified sum that Christ paid includes being willing to die, to take all the sin of the world upon him, to suffer, to have nails pierced in his hands and feet. He was crucified, buried and resurrected. The price that had to be paid to redeem us is found in Hebrews, Chapter 9.

I will share the plan of redemption according to my understanding. The Bible tells us that the high priest would offer a blood sacrifice for the errors of the people once a year. Verse one tells us that the first covenant had ordinances of divine service and a worldly sanctuary. In the tabernacle there was the candlestick, the table, and the showbread; which is called the sanctuary. Then after the second veil, the tabernacle which is called the Holiest of Holy had the golden censer and the ark of the covenant overlaid with gold, wherein was the golden pot that had manna, and Aaron's rod that budded and the tables of the covenant; and the cherubim's of glory shadowing the mercy seat. After this, the priests went into the first tabernacle, accomplishing the service of God.

But into the second veil, the high priest would go alone once every year, with blood, which he offered for himself and for the errors of the people. The Holy Ghost signified that the way into the Holiest of Holy was not yet made manifest, while the first tabernacle was still standing. Both gifts and sacrifices were offered that could not make him that did the service perfect, as pertained to the conscience; which stood only in meats and drinks, and divers washing, and carnal ordinances, imposed on them until the time of reformation.

Christ, came as the high priest of good things to come, by a greater and more perfect tabernacle, not made with hands, that is to say, not the building; neither by the blood of goats and calves, but by his own blood he entered in once into the holy place, having obtained eternal redemption for us. Hallelujah!

You see the blood of bulls and of goats, and the ashes of a heifer sprinkling the unclean, sanctifieth to the purifying of the flesh: HOW MUCH MORE shall the blood of Christ, who through the eternal Spirit offered himself without spot to God, purge your conscience from dead works to serve the living God? By the blood of Jesus offered on the mercy seat for our redemption, there was nothing missing and nothing lacking. The work was complete; the work of Christ is perfection! Now we can serve our living God. Jesus Christ paid the ultimate price for our redemption. Lord, blessed be your holy name.

Now, Jesus is the mediator of the New Testament. Jesus died for the redemption of the transgressions that were under the first testament, that they which are called might receive the promise of eternal inheritance. We have an eternal inheritance. It goes on throughout all eternity. Nothing is temporary in the work of Christ. It is completely and totally eternal. Eternal means to last or exist forever, without end or beginning. A few synonyms include everlasting, never-ending, abiding, permanent, enduring, infinite and timeless. Selah!

As you know, a testament is in force after men are dead; otherwise it is of no strength at all while they live. Even the first testament was dedicated with blood. When Moses had spoken every precept to all the people according to the law, he took the blood of calves and of goats, with water, and scarlet wool, and hyssop, and sprinkled the book, and all the people, saying, this is the blood of the testament which God hath enjoined unto you. He also sprinkled with blood both the tabernacle, and all the vessels of the ministry. Almost all things are by the law purged with blood; and without shedding of blood, there is no redemption.

You know that Christ is not entered into the holy places made with hands, which are the figures of the true; but into heaven itself, now to appear in the presence of God for us: Jesus is now in the presence of God for us! Jesus will never have to shed his blood again. Jesus does not ever have to offer himself again, like the high priest who had to enter into the holy place every year with the blood of others. Once and for all, Jesus has appeared to put away sin by the sacrifice of himself. Christ was offered to bear the sins of many. Christ will come again without sin unto salvation. Jesus is coming again. Jesus is returning for his children. Are you ready for his coming? His coming is very near!

The blood of Jesus was sinless and sacred. The blood shed on the cross was of God. There is a fountain filled with blood flowed from Immanuel's veins and sinners plunged beneath the flood lose all their guilty stain. Guilt and condemnation are not from God. The enemy and even sometimes our own flesh try to make us feel guilty and condemned. However, there is no condemnation to those who are in Christ Jesus. The law of the Spirit of life in Christ Jesus has set me free from the law of sin and death. God sees us through the blood of Jesus Christ and we take on the righteousness of our Lord and Savior Jesus Christ.

Therefore, we are no longer sin conscience, no longer shame conscience, no longer guilt conscience, but we are righteousness conscience. We are a new creation in Christ Jesus.

Isaiah 51:11 (AKJV): "Therefore the redeemed of the LORD shall return, and come with singing unto Zion; and everlasting joy *shall be* upon their head: they shall obtain gladness and joy; *and* sorrow and mourning shall flee away."

Let the redeemed of the Lord declare it today. I am redeemed! The blood of Jesus was not tainted by sin. The Savior must have pure and perfect blood. The Father of Jesus was the power of the Holy Spirit. None of the Adamic nature flowed through his veins. Jesus was spotless and without sin, but he took every sin we could ever commit upon himself so we could be redeemed, so we could be forgiven and be free in Christ. The blood of Jesus is perpetual; it never dries up. Our blood falls and dries up. The genuine real authentic blood of Jesus is on the mercy seat. The blood of Jesus gives us strength from day to day and it never loses its power!

In Galatians 3:13 from the Message Bible we read, "Christ redeemed us from that self-defeating, cursed life by absorbing it completely into himself." Do you remember the Scriptures that say, "Cursed is everyone who hangs on a tree"? That is what happened when Jesus was nailed to the cross: He became a curse, and at the same time dissolved the curse. And now, because of that, the air is cleared and we can see that Abraham's blessing is present and available for non-Jews, too. We are all able to receive God's life, His spirit, in and with us by believing—just the way Abraham received it.

Galatians 2:20 (AMP): "I have been crucified with Christ [in Him I have shared His crucifixion]; it is no longer I who live, but Christ (the Messiah) lives in me; and the life I now live in the body I live by faith in (by adherence to and reliance on and complete trust in) the Son of God, Who loved me and gave Himself up for me."

We must know that we were crucified, buried and resurrected with Christ and we are now seated with Christ in the heavenly places. WOW!! What blessed hope and faith. We know God's Word is true.

We have God's tremendous grace again in God's plan of redemption! My mind goes immediately to the scripture the Lord gave me for the beginning of His ministry through me. It begins in Titus 2:11 (KJV), "for the grace of God that brings salvation has appeared to all men. Teaching them that denying ungodliness and worldly lusts that we should live soberly, righteously, and godly in this present world. Looking for the blessed hope and glorious appearing of our great God and our Savior, Jesus Christ. "

Matthew 1:21-23 (NKJV): "And she will bring forth a Son, and you shall call His name JESUS, for He will save His people from their sins. So all this was done that it might be fulfilled which was spoken by the Lord through the prophet, saying: "Behold, the virgin shall be with child, and bear a Son, and they shall call His name Immanuel," which is translated, "God with us."

Redeemed, oh how I love to declare it, redeemed by the blood of the Lamb. The angel of the Lord told Mary in Luke 1:33 (NLT): " And he will reign over Israel forever; his Kingdom will never end!"

The plans of the enemy against Israel will not prevail because God will not allow Israel to be wiped out, because Jesus the Messiah will reign over Israel forever. Where Jesus reigns, grace prevails. Revelation 1:18 (KJV): "I am he that liveth, and was dead; and, behold, I am alive for evermore, Amen; and have the keys of hell and of death."

Aren't you glad Jesus is alive today? Aren't you glad that the grave could not hold Him? He lives today! He reigns and He rules today! He is Alpha, Omega, the beginning and the end. How do I know he lives? He lives within my heart!

When the scribes and the Pharisees were accusing Jesus of blaspheming, Jesus said to them in Matthew 9:4-8 (NKJV): "But Jesus, knowing their thoughts, said, "Why do you think evil in your hearts? For which is easier to say, Your sins are forgiven you, or to say arise and walk? But that you may know that the Son of Man has power on earth to forgive sins—then He said to the paralytic, "Arise, take up your bed, and go to your house." And he arose and departed to his house."

Then, why do we still bring up someone else's sin or even our own. Are we placing ourselves above God? My Jesus is the forgiving one. As Jesus was hanging on the cross, He asked God to forgive them because they did not know what they were doing. Church, we have to be in the forgiving and forgetting business. Jesus forgives us; we are to forgive others. Romans 4:7 (NKJV): "Blessed are those whose lawless deeds are forgiven and whose sins are covered."

Make yourself and others happy today and everyday by living a life of forgiveness and love.

1 John 1:8-10 (NKJV): "If we say that we have no sin, we deceive ourselves, and the truth is not in us. If we confess our sins, He is faithful and just to forgive us our sins and to cleanse us from all unrighteousness. If we say that we have not

sinned, we make Him a liar, and His word is not in us."

Through redemption, we have forgiveness of sins. Hallelujah!! Therefore, we are forever grateful.

1 John 2:2 (NKJV): "My little children, these things I write to you, so that you may not sin. And if anyone sins, we have an Advocate with the Father, Jesus Christ the righteous. And He Himself is the propitiation for our sins, and not for ours only but also for the whole world."

Propitiation means the turning away of wrath by an offering. When Jesus died on the cross, he turned away the wrath of God! His blood sacrifice made God well pleased. For we know, without the shedding of blood, there is no remission of sins.

John 19:28-30 (NKJV): "After this, Jesus, knowing that all things were now accomplished, that the Scripture might be fulfilled, said, "I thirst!" Now a vessel full of sour wine was sitting there, and they filled a spoon with sour wine, put it on hyssop and put it to His mouth. So when Jesus had received the sour wine, He said, "It is finished!" and bowing His head, He gave up His spirit."

We cannot do one thing to add to the plan of salvation. God's redemption is at Christ's expense. I have good news. Jesus died for you, for your children, for your grandchildren. Choose to follow Christ today as we have learned again that the Word of the Lord shall prevail! If the Bible says we have been redeemed, it is true and the Word shall prevail. If the Word says, we are forgiven, then we are forgiven. Do not let anyone steal the Word of God from your heart and your mind. SSSSSSSH! The Word of the Lord shall prevail!

Matthew 16:18 (TLB): "You are Peter, a stone; and upon this rock I will build my church; and all the powers of hell shall not prevail against it."

Hebrews 12:2 (NKJV): "Looking unto Jesus, the author and finisher of our faith, who for the joy that was set before Him endured the cross, despising the shame, and has sat down at the right hand of the throne of God."

You are the apple of God's eye. God loves you!

Philippians 1:6 (NKJV): "being confident of this very thing that He who has begun a good work in you will complete it until they day of Jesus Christ."

When Christ returns, he will return without sin for salvation. Until then, let's follow John 4:34 (TLB): Then Jesus explained: "My nourishment comes from doing the will of God who sent me, and from finishing his work."

To know God in His plan of redemption is to be well equipped here on the earth to walk in the abundant life we have been summoned to by God himself.

It is very important that we never forget God's plan for redeeming mankind. One way we can remember is to partake of the Lord's Supper. As often as we partake, we are to remember the Lord's death until he comes.

The Lord's Supper is a powerful proclamation. 1 Corinthians 11:26 (NKJV) : "For as often as you eat this bread and drink this cup, you proclaim the Lord's death till He comes." In Matthew 26:26-28 (NKJV) "And as they were eating, Jesus took bread, blessed and broke it, and gave it to the disciples and said, "Take, eat; this is My body." Then He took the cup, and gave thanks, and gave it to them, saying, "Drink from it, all of you. For this is My Blood of the new covenant, which is shed for many for the remission of sins." The Lord's Supper is our vital identification with Christ our Lord and Savior.

Heavenly Father, thank you so much for sending Your only begotten Son, full of grace and truth for us. Thank you that while we were yet sinners, Christ died for us. Thank you, Father, for your grace in redeeming us and now we are called the people of God. Once we were not a people, but now we are the people of God called by your name, called out of darkness into your marvelous light. We are one holy race, because of the blood of Jesus, your precious son. Immanuel, God with us!

CHAPTER 6

SSSSSSSH!
Knowing God's Grace to Reign as Kings in life through Jesus Christ

Heavenly Father, we pray that your Word will go forth unhindered. We pray that your Word will go into the good soil of the hearts of the people and not one person will leave here the way they came in Jesus' name. Father God, we thank you for your glorious grace. Holy Spirit, you are our teacher and our comforter. We thank you for teaching and comforting us, in the name of Jesus Christ of Nazareth, Amen.

I have been teaching that because we know God and because we know God's Word is true, that The Word of the Lord shall prevail. Even when we are being bombarded with bad thoughts, even when our bodies are screaming in pain, even when we have to literally tell ourselves to be quiet, we can rest assured God is on the throne and God's Word will win in our lives and in the lives of others. If we only believe, all things are possible.

I want to show you that we can reign as kings in this life through Jesus Christ. The Word of the Lord shall prevail! Therefore, we quiet our minds and our hearts and meditate on the Word of God.

Grace is brought to all of us by the revelation of Jesus Christ. God wants us to grow in the grace and knowledge of our Lord and Savior. A vine growing on a wall will die without a solid root, good light and sufficient water. It is also true that without a solid root in Christ and without the light of the Word, we would shrivel up spiritually. We must have deep tap roots. Just like our bodies need proper nourishment, so likewise our spirits need proper nourishment. The Bible says that he who hungers and thirsts after righteousness shall be filled. Let us never lose our hunger for God and for the Bible.

How about the grace that God has given us to reign as kings in this life? Now, faith is the victory that overcomes the world.

As Christians, we need to draw on, live by, and count on the abundance of grace that grants us, as believers, to reign over life. We are to reign in life. We cannot be victorious Christ-like overcomers, if we lack knowledge of and trust in the abundance of grace God offers. Those of us who receive the abundance of grace are those who reign in this life. The reason is found in Romans 5:17 (NKJV) "For if by the one man's offense death reigned through the one, much more those who receive abundance of grace and of the gift of righteousness will reign in life through the One, Jesus Christ." Also I like the NLT translation which says, "For the sin of this one man Adam caused death to rule over many but EVEN GREATER is God's wonderful grace and his gift of righteousness for all who receive it will live in **triumph** over sin and death through the one man Jesus Christ."

One time the Lord told me that I would never come to maturity as long as I blamed people for all of my problems. He told me that He has given me the authority to reign as a king in this life. He said that as soon as I begin to take responsibility for all of my decisions, I would become mature. Since that revelation, that has been my goal. Thus, I had to forgive a lot of people and set them free. Whom the Son sets free is free indeed. Sometimes we have people locked in the prison of our minds. Let them go, set them free, forgive them. Begin to reign as a king in your life through Jesus Christ. My life has been truly changed since this encounter with the Lord.

The Bible tells us in 1 Corinthians 15:57-58 (NKJV) "But thanks be to God, who gives us the victory through our Lord Jesus Christ. Therefore, my beloved brethren, be steadfast, immovable, always abounding in the work of the Lord, knowing that your labor is not in vain in the Lord." When you serve the Lord, your labor is not in vain and the Word of the Lord shall prevail!

We grow in the knowledge of our Lord by studying His Word. We know that Jesus is the Word. Jesus is the Way, the Truth and the Life. How can be boldly and confidently say SSSSSSSH! The Word of the Lord Shall Prevail? We can say that precisely because we KNOW GOD!

1 Corinthians 2:12-14 (NKJV): "Now we have received, not the spirit of the world, but the Spirit who is from God, that we might know the things that have been freely given to us by God. These things we also speak, not in words which man's wisdom teaches but which the Holy Spirit teaches, comparing spiritual things with spiritual. But the natural man does not receive the things of the Spirit of God, for they are foolishness to him; nor can he know *them,* because they are spiritually discerned." As Christians, when we are born again, we receive the mind of Christ.

Growing in Grace is learning more about God and Jesus Christ and the Holy Spirit—Our Blessed Trinity. To know God is to love Him and become intimately acquainted with Him. Growing in grace is not becoming more saved than at the moment of conversion. For when we are saved, we are made the righteousness of God in Christ Jesus our Lord. When we are saved, we become a new creation. I suppose my Mother taught me more about grace than anyone in my growing-up years. She raised 15 children so one can only imagine that without the grace of God, she would not have been successful. However, she applied grace to her life every day. When one of her children would begin acting up/misbehaving, she would pull on her Pentecostal hairdo and pray loudly, "Lord, give me grace." She would say this several times. Immediately the presence of God and his grace would fill the room and every child became silent.

My Mother was in a covenant with God and she appropriated all the benefits as needed. I remember being with her and quoting Psalm 103:1-5. You can look it up, but especially in the midst of my need I would say. God forgives all my iniquities. God heals all my diseases. God redeems my life from destruction. God crowns me with loving kindness and tender mercies. God satisfies my mouth with good things so that my youth is renewed as an eagle. Yes I will bless the Lord at all times. My Dad, as well, was a role model for Jesus. He was always blessing the Lord at home, in the community and on his job.

God has a blood covenant with us and he has given us everything that pertains to life and godliness. He took our sin to give us His righteousness. He took our poverty, and he meets all our needs in glory by Christ Jesus. Whenever God asks us to do something, he provides all we need to accomplish his order. If God has already given us everything that pertains to life and godliness, then we need to receive it by faith. Then we can truly REIGN in life NOW. We reign in life through righteousness because we choose to. God gave us one life to live and we will individually answer on judgment day. We cannot blame our Mom, our Dad, our teachers, our friends, not anyone. However, there will be times when we must be still and quiet our own minds and cast down every thought that exalts itself against the knowledge of God and declare, "The Word of the Lord shall prevail."

Listen, God's grace is given to each of us. Let us now look at someone who walked in grace, who reigned in grace in the midst of wickedness, in the midst of evil doings.

The story is found in 1 Samuel 25. This story is about a woman named Abigail. Abigail was a beautiful woman, full of wisdom. She was a woman full of grace and knew how to reign in life through righteousness. I love to read the story about Abigail.

However, Abigail was married to a man named Nabal, who was rough and evil in his walk. Now, there was a time when Nabal had his men shearing sheep. David took this as an opportunity to have his men go in peace to see Nabal and tell Nabal that David had sent them. David was hoping that Nabal would provide food, etc., for his men. David told his men to ask Nabal to let them find favor (grace) in his sight.

The story goes on that they did exactly what David said to do. However, Nabal said, "Who is David, and who is the son of Jesse?" He was so busy building up his own fortune and doing his own thing that he hadn't taken time to get to know David. Nabal had no knowledge that David was the one who killed Goliath and that David was chosen to be King.

Nevertheless, Nabal refused to give David's men anything. Do you think David was upset when the men told him what happened? If you said yes, you are correct. He was "fit to be tied."

Let us go now to 1 Samuel 25:13 (NKJV) "Then David said to his men, "Every man gird on his sword." So every man girded on his sword, and David also girded on his sword. And about four hundred men went with David and two hundred stayed with the supplies.'

Now remember that earlier David had protected all that Nabal had so that nothing was missed of all that belonged to Nabal. Let us look at 1 Samuel 25:21-22 (NKJV) "Now David had said "Surely in vain I have protected all that this fellow has in the wilderness, so that nothing was missed of all that belongs to him. And he has repaid me evil for good. May God do so, and more also, to the enemies of David, if I leave one male of all who belong to him by morning light."
I would say that David flew into a tirade. He was extremely angry.

Shortly afterward one of Nabal's young men told Abigail everything. Abigail decided to reign as a king in her life and rule in the grace God had given to her. She decided to go to David herself and ask for mercy for her husband and for all the men.

When Abigail saw David, she got off her donkey and fell before David on her face and did obeisance. Kneeling at his feet, she said, "Place this guilt on me and let your handmaid speak in your presence and hear me." Those words of grace flowed right off her lips. She pleaded with David. She asked that the gifts she brought to David's men be given to them. She told David that evil had **not** been found in him all his days. She told him that his battles were the Lord's battles. She said the Lord will make you ruler over Israel. She only spoke what she knew God had said. Likewise, we need only to speak what God has said.

She asked David to remember her after God had dealt with Nabal. David said to Abigail, as I hear grace flowing from his lips. 1 Samuel 35:32-35 (NKJV) "Blessed is the Lord God of Israel, who sent you this day to meet me! And blessed is your advice and blessed are you, because you have kept me this day from coming to bloodshed and from avenging myself with my own hand. For indeed, as the Lord of Israel lives, who has kept me back from hurting you, unless you had hurried and come to meet me, surely by morning light no males would have been left to Nabal!" "So David received from her hand what she had brought him, and said to her, "Go up in peace to your house. See, I have heeded your voice and respected your person."

Next, Abigail went back home and Nabal was holding a feast and he was drunk. Like a wise woman knows, you don't try to reason with a drunk man. BUT, in the morning Abigail told Nabal what had happened and his heart died within him and became as stone. Hard hearted! Ten days after that the Lord smote Nabal and he died.

David was God's man and God gave grace to David through Abigail. David acknowledged God as leading Abigail. Always give God all the glory for it is His abundance of grace that keeps us. Let this story also be a reminder to us to obey God when he tells you to do something. Obey God in a timely manner, when he has spoken to you. Being at the right place at the right time is very important. Let us follow the leading of the Lord in our lives and be quick to obey. Abigail's obedience to quickly obey the word of the Lord caused the Word of God to prevail in David's life. Hallelujah! Glory to God!

Can you believe that after David heard that Nabal had died, he sent his servant to ask Abigail to be his wife? Grace! Grace! Grace!

Now, let us consider the grace of God upon Abigail's life. She chose to walk in grace even though her husband was evil. She chose to communicate with David. She took the time to know David. She asked David for grace toward her wicked husband, Nabal. She extended great faith toward David and his men (Imagine approaching 400 men and David who were girded with swords.) She chose to do what was good, right and true. She reigned in life by grace through righteousness and was successful. The blood of her husband and servants was not on her hands nor David's hands.

God has given to each of us his amazing grace to reign as kings in life through Jesus Christ. Our choices determine our destiny. Abigail's choice that day determined her destiny and she not only reigned as a king that day but she was chosen to marry David. Selah!

God has called us up to a level of grace, and we do not have to step down for any person or any devil. Stay humble before God. Let us humble ourselves under the mighty hand of God and he will exalt us in due time.

We can walk in grace no matter what our surroundings are, on the job, on the road, in our homes, in stores, with family and with children and grandchildren.

This is an exhortation to take charge of your decisions. Take responsibility for your decisions. You are only responsible for your own actions.

You are God's child and God loves you and has a great destiny for you. I am sure Abigail had no idea of her destiny before she made a choice to do what was right that day. So, even if you do not know your destiny yet, just continue to follow God and obey his voice every day.

Make a decision that today you will cast down every imagination and every bad thought that exalts itself against the knowledge of God. Take captive every thought to the obedience of Christ. Walk in love today and the evil one will not touch you. Greater is God who is in us than he who is in the world. We can do all things through Christ who strengthens us. We are more than conquerors.

Father, in the name of Jesus, we thank you for your Word. We agree with your Word that it will not return void to you, but it will accomplish what you sent it to accomplish. May everyone be changed to walk and live in your grace, surrounded by your love and protection, in Jesus' name, Amen.

Chapter 7

SSSSSSSH! Knowing God's Word

1 Peter 1:25 (NKJV) declares, But the Word of the Lord shall endure forever. We believe that the Word of the Lord shall prevail because God's word is a sure foundation.

Heavenly Father, we pray that your Word will accomplish exactly what desire. May we not only have more knowledge about your Word but grow into more of an intimacy with you and your will for our lives. We long to know the width, length, depth and height of your love. Be magnified in our midst now! Holy Spirit, you are welcome in this place. Father you are our Father and you are full of mercy and grace. You are welcome in this place, in Jesus' name, Amen.

I said in the beginning that we can boldly and confidently say, "SSSSSSSH! The Word of the Lord Shall Prevail" because we KNOW God. To know God means that we will look to God and our expectations will be from God alone. Psalm 62:5 (KJV): "My soul wait thou only upon God, for my expectation is from Him."

I want to focus on God's desire for us in seven specific areas.   I always like to sing this song of love with the Lord. I will share the words with you now.

Lord, to know, know, know you is to love, love, love you.

Just to see you smile makes my life worthwhile.

To know, know, know you is to love, love, love you and I do.

Yes I do. Yes we do.

Remember the reason I want to share the Word is because I was in bondage to the world until I started devouring God's Word. I have seen how reading, meditating, memorizing, and knowing God's Word has brought me into God's Promise Land. I was blind, but now I can see. I was lost, but now I am found. God gave me the following song in the early 80's:

It's the Word that brought me up.

It's the Word that brought me out.

It's the Word. It's the Word. It's the Word.

So, I must share it with you and then

Watch What God will do.

It's the Word. It's the Word. It's the Word.

For I know when it goes forth from the south, east, west, or north

That the God who reigns on high.

He will hear you. He will heal you. He will answer when you cry.

It's the Word. It's the Word. It's the Word.

His Word is burning in my heart, from His Word I can't depart,

For I've served self and watched Satan steal and kill.

And I know that it's far better to be in the Father's will.

It's the Word. It's the Word. It's the Word.

In other words, I want to encourage you to put knowing God the Father, Son and Holy Spirit and knowing His Word to be an utmost priority in your life. Life is in the word because it is sharp and powerful as we know.

Let's look at the seven specific areas that we can focus on for knowing God in a greater dimension than ever before and knowing God's will for us:

I.   God's Word concerning the manifestation of the sons of God.

Galatians 4:7 (KJV): "And because ye are sons, God hath sent forth the Spirit of his Son into your hearts, crying, Abba, Father. Wherefore thou art no more a servant, but a son; and if a son, then an heir of God through Christ."

1 John 3:2-3 (KJV): "Beloved, now are we the sons of God, and it doth not yet appear what we shall be: but we know that, when he shall appear, we shall be like him; for we shall see him as he is. And every man that hath this hope in him purifieth himself, even as he is pure."

The first time I learned about the manifestation of the sons of God, I was with my Dad while he was in the hospital fighting cancer of the lungs, which he contacted from working in the coal mines. That morning, the Holy Spirit gave me the scriptures for us to study. We studied Romans, Chapter 8. Romans 8:18-23 (NKJV): "For I consider that the sufferings of this present time are not worthy to be compared with the glory which shall be revealed in us. For the earnest expectation of the creation eagerly waits for the revealing of the sons of God. For the creation was subjected to futility, not willingly but because of Him who subjected it in hope; because the creation itself also will be delivered from the bondage of corruption into the glorious liberty of the children of God. For we know that the whole creation groans and labors with birth pangs together until now. Not only that but we also who have the first fruits of the Spirit, even we ourselves groan within ourselves, eagerly waiting for the adoption, the redemption of our body."

In Verse 23, does that mean we wait for the redemption of our bodies because we have to go the grave first? Are we correct to say that our spirits are redeemed when we receive salvation, but our bodies wait for redemption should we go by the grave? 1 Corinthians 15:52-53 (NKJV): "In a moment, in the twinkling of an eye, at the last trumpet. For the trumpet will sound, and the dead will be raised incorruptible, and we shall be changed. For this corruptible must put on incorruption, and this mortal must put on immortality. "

We will be raised imperishable, which means free and immune from decay. Jesus purchased your glorified body through his death, burial and resurrection. Although full payment has been made, you still have a corrupted body while you wait to receive your immortal incorruptible one. At this moment you don't yet have the redemption of the purchased possession.

According to God's Word, we are to become the manifest sons of God. How will people know who we are if we are not letting our light shine for Jesus? My Dad and Mom both certainly let their light shine for Jesus and they were not ashamed of the gospel of Christ. I remember giggling under my breath once when we ate out, because Dad prayed so loudly for God to bless our food.

Wherever we are, do we boldly make a stand for Christ? Let us always stand up for the gospel of Christ. Can other people know we are Christians by the love we have for them? Yes, they certainly can know that we are Christians by our love.

My prayer for you is that you would know the hope of your calling, the hope of becoming the visible manifest sons and daughters of God in this present world.

The whole earth is groaning for YOU! You are the manifest sons of God! All of creation groans for you to fulfill your destiny as a manifest son of God!!

We are the children of God. The whole creation is groaning for you to be manifested that you might take your authority that God has given to you and destroy the works of the devil by following after Christ, walking in His Word, and taking the gospel to your family and to every living creature, that the works of the devil (sin, lawlessness, disobedience, carnality, error, apostasy, discord, missing the mark) will be dissolved, destroyed and Satan will have to lose his hold on you and everything that pertains to you. Through our God, we shall do well. We have victory in Jesus.

Say: *I choose to become visible to my family, and to all those around me that I have been delivered from the bondage of corruption into the glorious liberty of the children of God. I choose to become visible to anyone who comes in contact with me. I am a child of the King and I am a spirit. I walk in the favor of God. I am not ashamed of the gospel of Christ for it is the power of God unto salvation.*

II.   God's Word concerning keeping our eyes and minds on Christ Jesus

Our key scripture is Hebrews 12:2 (KJV): "Looking unto Jesus, the author and finisher of our faith, who for the joy that was set before him endured the cross, despising the shame and has set down at the right hand of the throne of God."

Why do we want to keep our eyes and minds on Christ Jesus? 2 Corinthians 2:14 (KJV) says we always triumph in Christ. Of course, we want to keep our eyes and minds on Christ Jesus. We all love to triumph!

The definition of look is to turn one's eyes toward something in order to see. Also, it means to use one's sight or vision in seeking to face. To keep means to hold or to retain in one's possession and to hold in a given place. The world is not the place to seek help for keeping our eyes on Jesus. We are to turn our eyes toward Jesus and look closely into his wonderful face. Then, the things that are bothering us will slowly fade away. We will see the victory no matter what the circumstances. Halleujah!

The NIV version of Hebrews 12:2 says, "Let us fix our eyes." To fix as a verb is to implant an image firmly in a person's mind. 2 Corinthians 4:6 (NJKV): "For it is the God who commanded light to shine out of darkness, who has shone in our hearts to give the light of the knowledge of the glory of God in the face of Jesus Christ."

As born-again believers, we want to keep our eyes and minds upon Jesus. 2 Corinthians 3:18 (KJV): "But we all with open face beholding as in a glass the glory of the Lord, even as by the Spirit of the Lord." I love being changed from one glory to the next. Do you like it, too?

John the Baptist is a great example of someone who looked and kept his mind on Christ Jesus. He came to prepare the way of the Lord.

John 1:29-37 (KJV): "The next day John seeth Jesus coming unto him, and saith, Behold the Lamb of God, which taketh away the sin of the world. This is he of whom I said, After me cometh a man which is preferred before me: for he was before me. And I knew him not: but that he should be made manifest to Israel, therefore am I come baptizing with water. And John bare record, saying, I saw the Spirit descending from heaven like a dove, and it abode upon him. And I knew him not: but he that sent me to baptize with water, the same said unto me, Upon whom thou shalt see the Spirit descending, and remaining on him, the same is he which baptizeth with the Holy Ghost. And I saw, and bare record that this is the Son of God. Again the next day after John stood, and two of his disciples; And looking upon Jesus as he walked, he saith, Behold the Lamb of God! And the two disciples heard him speak, and they followed Jesus."

John the Baptist truly kept his life focused on Jesus. He focused on looking at the author and finisher of his faith. The good news is that it is Jesus who has begun a good work in us and it is Jesus who will finish the good work in us. Our desire is to continually stay focused on Jesus Christ.

In order to keep our eyes and our minds on Christ Jesus, we must live out of our spirit. Christ in us is our hope of glory. Our born-again spirit is right now as perfect, mature, and complete as Jesus himself. What is in your spirit must flow through your soul in order to get out to your body and the physical world around it. Your spirit is your life-giving part. You have the resurrection life of God in your spirit.

I was having problems with snoring, so my doctor ordered a sleep apnea test. During a sleep apnea test in the hospital, my spirit was singing all night. Prior to going to the hospital, I attended corporate prayer at church. I asked my Pastor to pray for me before I left for the test. My Pastor laid hands on me and prayed in the Spirit. God's presence became so tangible to my spirit, which in turn ministered to my heart and mind. That night the nurses were very frustrated because I could not go to sleep. There is life in your spirit now, once you receive Christ into your heart. My spirit was more alive that night than anything else. During the middle of the night, a demonic influence hovered over my bed and the demon spoke and said, "Why don't you commit suicide?" I was so full of God's Word and my spirit was so full of life that I just rolled over and gave it no credence. Early the next morning, they let me know that I could leave and they were not happy with me.

The next week, the doctor called and said that as long as I slept on my right side, I would snore very little. My husband, Rusty, and I teamed up to make it work. He very gently touches me if I have moved from my right side and immediately I readjust. Teamwork makes the dream work, and I give God all of the glory.

The law of the spirit of life in Christ Jesus has made us free from the law of sin and death. Jesus has come that we might have life and have it more abundantly.

The Christian life is a process of renewing my mind with the Word of God and living out of my spirit. Galatians 5:22-23 (NKJV) "But the fruit of the Spirit is love, joy, peace, longsuffering, kindness, goodness, faithfulness, gentleness, self-control. Against such there is no law." Galatians 5:25(NKJV): "if we live in the Spirit, let us also walk in the Spirit." We are to acknowledge every good thing that is in us in Christ Jesus.

Romans 8:6-10 (NKJV): "For to be carnally minded is death, but to be spiritually minded is life and peace. Because the carnal mind is enmity against God; for it is not subject to the law of God, nor indeed can be. So then, those who are in the flesh cannot please God. But you are not in the flesh but in the Spirit, if indeed the Spirit of God dwells in you. Now if anyone does not have the Spirit of Christ, he is not His. And if Christ is in you, the body is dead because of sin, but the Spirit is life because of righteousness."

The number one way to keep your mind stayed on the Lord is to read the Bible, pray every day and you will grow in Christ.

The Bible tells us that we are to look unto Jesus the author and the finisher of our faith who for the joy that was set before him, endured the cross, suffered the shame and is now seated at the right hand of the Father. If we keep our eyes upon Jesus, others will not take His place.

Beloved, now we are the sons of God and God has great plans for us. I pray that your perfect and mature spirit would flow through your soul in order to get out to your body and the physical world. I pray that we would become a holy vessel of God. Our spirit is the life-giving part. We must renew our minds with God's word, so that the fruit of the Spirit can permeate our minds.

III. God's Word concerning our intimacy with Him

How do we accomplish knowing God? How do we accomplish becoming more intimate with God? Is God really number one in our lives? God is a jealous God and he says he will have no other gods before HIM. What is a very important part of knowing God? Keeping our eyes upon Jesus.

The Bible teaches us that the only way we can pray to our Father in heaven is in the name of Jesus. With Jesus and his blood sacrifice on Calvary's tree, we have access to the Father. There is one true God and He is the Father of our Lord Jesus Christ. By Jesus's completed work in his death, burial, and resurrection, we have access to go to our Heavenly Father.

If we want to become more intimate with someone, it requires that we spend time with them. If we want to become more intimate with God, it requires we spend time with HIM. If we keep our minds stayed on God, we will have supernatural peace. Isaiah 26:3 (NKJV): "You will keep *him* in perfect peace, *Whose* mind *is* stayed *on You,* Because he trusts in You."

When you focus on Jesus, everyone else gets to see Him too. That is what happened with John the Baptist because John focused on Jesus. In John 3:26-30 (NKJV): "And they came to John and said to him, "Rabbi, He who was with you beyond the Jordan, to whom you have testified—behold, He is baptizing, and all are coming to Him!" John answered and said, "A man can receive nothing unless it has been given to him from heaven. You yourselves bear me witness, that I said, 'I am not the Christ,' but, 'I have been sent before Him.' He who has the bride is the bridegroom; but the friend of the bridegroom, who stands and hears him, rejoices greatly because of the bridegroom's voice. Therefore this joy of mine is fulfilled. He must increase, but I *must* decrease."

As born-again believers, we want to keep our eyes upon Jesus.

Keeping our eyes upon Jesus is:

1. A lifetime exercise
2. A focus that will cost you because sometimes you have to go alone.
3. A Choice
4. Knowing where you keep looking is where you will go.
5. Knowing it will affect your relationship with Jesus and others.
6. Knowing you will have supernatural peace and joy.
7. Knowing you will fulfill your destiny.

God wants you to keep your eyes upon Jesus and He will help you do this. Philippians 1:6 (KJV): "Being confident of this very thing that he who has began a good work in you will be faithful to complete it." Our part is surrender and obedience. The Holy Spirit helps us to keep looking to Jesus. The Holy Spirit doesn't talk about himself; he talks about Jesus.

John the Baptist was sent to prepare the way of the Lord. We are sent to bring people to Christ. This is our primary purpose. We are saved by grace through faith. Because of everything that

God did at Christ's expense, we believe in Jesus and receive Him into our hearts.

John 3:16 (KJV): "For God so loved the world that He gave his only begotten Son that whosoever believeth in Him should not perish but have everlasting life."

To become intimate with God, we need to know once and for all that God is love. We need to know that God loves us. We need to know that God heals and God heals us. God is good all the time.

God is looking for a pure heart. Philippians 4:8 (KJV): "Finally, brethren, whatsoever things are true, whatsoever things are honest, whatsoever things are just, whatsoever things are pure, whatsoever things are lovely, whatsoever things are of good report; if there be any virtue, and if there be any praise, think on these things."

God loves to be praised. Did you know that Praise to God silences the enemy? We are saying SHUT UP to the devil when we praise God! Jesus told the devil, It is WRITTEN! We need to follow his examples.

There is nothing sweeter than spending time with God in prayer. It is true that every hour we spend in prayer is sweet.

Our Heavenly Father, our Savior Jesus Christ and the Holy Spirit are one in three and three in one. The Holy Spirit is always pointing to Jesus, and Jesus is always pointing to God.

In order to become more intimate with God, we must:

1. Keep our eyes upon Jesus.
2. Spend time with God.
3. Spend time reading the Bible.
4. Keep our minds stayed on God.
5. Praise God.
6. Pray.
7. Minister to the Lord for all His goodness.

Say:

I will bless the Lord at all times; His praise shall continually be in my mouth.

I will keep my eyes upon Jesus.

I will spend time in God's Word.

I will spend time with God.

I will keep my mind stayed on God so I will have supernatural peace.

I will praise God morning, noon and night.

IV. God's Word concerning healing

When I was in the wilderness of suffering, I wrongly thought because my sin was so bad that the Lord would not and could not heal me. During that time, my sister Debi, on instructions from the Lord, came to visit me. She asked me one question which changed my life forever. She asked me, "Betty, is the blood of Jesus enough?" With tears in my eyes, and thankfulness in my heart I replied, "Yes." It was truly a word from the Lord that day. Right then I knew it was God's will to heal and it was God's will to heal me. It had always been easy for me to believe for other's healing, but it was difficult to believe for my own healing. I knew how powerful the blood of Jesus is, but I had forgotten that it was powerful in my very own life.

It is surely true that one word from God can change your life forever and it happened to me that very day. Remember that we are not to trust in the arm of the flesh, but we are to trust in the arm of the Lord. We trust in what God has said and what God has ordained. I remembered how I had gotten to that point. Some "so called" Christian brother had told me that God could forgive my sins but that he could not forgive my iniquities. It grieved my spirit because of the negative word that was given to me. For the duration of that sickness, in order to overcome that negative word, I meditated and memorized the Word of the Lord that would prevail in my life. That Word is found in Psalm 103:1-5 (NKJV): "Bless the Lord, O my soul: And all that is within me bless His holy name! Bless the Lord, O my soul, and forget not all His benefits: Who forgives all your iniquities, Who heals all your diseases, Who redeems your life from destruction, Who crowns you with loving kindness and tender mercies. Who satisfies your mouth with good things So that your youth is renewed like the eagles." I meditated and memorized this scripture. No one could ever deceive me again concerning God's word that he forgives ALL my iniquities, and heals ALL my diseases. Just a side note, which is why it is so important that we read the Bible for ourselves and allow the Holy Spirit to teach us, concerning

God's Word. No one is infallible, only the Word of God is infallible.

Another time, someone told me that God was not with me because I was too full of myself. That made me so sad that I cried and cried. I never wanted God to take his Holy Spirit from me or leave me Himself. I could not stomach the thought that God was not with me. How I had forgotten the scripture that says God will never leave us or forsake us amazes me! However, some time later I remembered and said, "Shut up, Betty. The Word of the Lord says that God will NEVER leave us or forsake us. He did not leave you and he will never leave you!"

I found the scripture that says God will even hold my right hand and He never lets go of our hand. One of my Dad's favorite songs was, "Precious Lord, take my hand." As a matter of fact, on his tombstone the hands of Jesus are engraved.

Two of my favorite scriptures for healing are Isaiah 53:5 and 1 Peter 2:24.

What I truly learned while being in the wilderness is it is always God's will to heal, and it is always God's will to heal me. Many times, I do not understand why some people are not healed. However, that is really not our business, it is up to God. God tells us to pray for people to be healed, but God is their healer. We are to pray and believe and God heals. There are many more scriptures on healing alone. These are just a few of my favorite scriptures on healing.

V. God's Word for walking in love

1st Corinthians 13:1-13 (NKJV): "Though I speak with the tongues of men and of angels, but have not love, I have become sounding brass or a clanging cymbal. And though I have the gift of prophecy, and understand all mysteries and all knowledge, and though I have all faith, so that I could remove mountains, but have not love, I am nothing. And though I have all faith, so that I could remove mountains, but have not love, I am nothing. And though I bestow all my goods to feed the poor, and though I give my body to be burned, but have not love, it profits me nothing. Love suffers long and is kind, love does not envy, love does not parade itself, is not puffed up; does not behave rudely, does not seek its own, is not provoked, thinks no evil; does not rejoice in iniquity, but rejoices in the truth; bears all things, believes all things, hopes all things, endures all things. Love never fails, but whether there are prophecies, they will fail, whether there are tongues, they will cease; whether there is knowledge it will vanish away. For we know in part and we prophesy in part. But when that which is perfect has come, then that which is in part will be done away. When I was a child, I spoke as a child, I understood as a child, I thought as a child; but when I became a man, I put away childish things. For now we see in a mirror, dimly, but then face to face. Now I know in part, but then I shall know just as I also am known. And now abide faith, hope, love, these three, but the greatest of these is love."

In the heart of God, He makes it clear that the greatest thing in all the world is to walk in love. God is love and without God there is no love. Even if we have the faith to remove mountains, it is zero, unless we let love rule. I remember so well how my Mom and Dad walked in love. They were definitely the manifest sons of God in the love walk, as well as many other areas. Where love abounds, grace abounds. The Lord told me that when I teach His Word I will be in His grace, surrounded by His Love. God's Love is the safest place in the world.

VI. God's Word for forgiveness

The Bible is very clear about God's stand on walking in forgiveness.

The scripture is found in Matthew 6:14-15 (NKJV): " For if you forgive men their trespasses, your heavenly Father will also forgive you. But if you do not forgive men their trespasses, neither will your Father forgive your trespasses." There are no ifs, ands, or butts. However, you can locate people right away when they have unforgiveness toward someone. They will have every excuse in the world for not forgiving that person. Rusty Kemper, my husband, taught me when we first got married how important this Word is in our lives. I needed to be reminded because I had to forgive those who had harmed me. Look what Jesus did. He told His Heavenly Father to forgive all those people who nailed him to the cross. He told God that they really did not know what they were doing. I think it is also true with people, sometimes they do know but sometimes they are unaware of how cruel they can be to other people.

114

Now, I know the scripture and therefore, I must forgive. The Lord also taught me that if it is too hard for me to forgive, I say Jesus please forgive that person through me. He also taught me to not only forgive them, but to ask the Lord to heal me of the hurt that was inflicted upon me through their bitterness toward me. Now I pray, Lord I forgive so and so and I ask you to cleanse me from the defilement that got on me through their offense. Another way that we overcome is to immediately say, "I will not be offended in the name of Jesus." We do not take the offense and no forgiveness is needed. I like that!

VII. God's Word concerning faith

We are to have faith in God! The God kind of faith will not work in an unforgiving heart. Mark 11:25-26 (NKJV): "And when ye stand praying, forgive, if ye have ought against any; that your Father also which is in heaven may forgive you your trespasses. But if ye do not forgive, neither will your Father which is in heaven forgive your trespasses." Faith in God and walking in God's love and forgiveness work hand in hand.

Galatians 5:6 (KJV): "For in Jesus Christ neither circumcision availeth anything, nor uncircumcision; but faith which worketh by love." Show me your love and I will see your faith in action. You know that Satan may put doubt in your mind, but the Word will put faith in your heart. The highest form of faith is faith in the Word of God. Did you know that love makes faith work at its highest level?

Hebrews 11:6 (KVJ): "But without faith it is impossible to please him; for he that cometh to God must believe that he is, and that he is a rewarder of them that diligently seek him."

Mark 11:23 (KJV) "For verily I say unto you That whosoever shall say unto this mountain, Be thou removed, and be cast into the sea; and shall not doubt in his heart, but shall believe that those things which he saith shall come to pass; he shall have whatsoever he saith." Your faith truly makes you whole.

We know that the Word of the Lord shall prevail. We have the highest form of faith because we believe God's Word is true. We are willing to command our minds and our bodies to be still and line up with the word of God. We confess God's Word in every situation. We do not trust in the arm of the flesh, but we trust in the Lord.

My exhortation to you today is SSSSSSSH! The Word of the Lord Shall Prevail in your life. God loves you. God will heal you. God will deliver you. God would have sent his son Jesus to die just for you if you were the only one on the earth. You are precious and very valuable. You are the apple of God's eye.

May God's peace, which passes all understanding, keep your hearts and minds in Christ Jesus at all times. Know that grace and mercy follow YOU all the days of your lives. Be encouraged! God loves you and so do I.

Precious Father, we worship you. WE praise you. We thank you for sending Jesus that we might have access to you. You, who created the sun the moon and the stars. You, who made us in your own image and after your likeness. You, who knew us even before we were formed in our Mother's womb. We are so hungry to know you more, Lord! To you be all glory, honor and praise, in Jesus name, Amen.

A copy for a friend?

https://www.createspace.com/5586731

Made in the USA
Charleston, SC
08 August 2015